text me

:-) HHOJ
d:-) *:-) @
:-(SMO
ABO:-) HHOJ Luv :-1 BK OTT WON
d: B-) :@
:-(WOT
AB IT WOM
d: B-) :@
:-(WOT
AB IT WOM
{yo IOJ Lu
:/ %-) GR
BK :o) TI
ou} Luv :
:/ O %-) GR
BK :o) TI
ou} J Luv :
:/ OH WOT R :-) d:-) *:-) %-) GR
BK OTT WOM :-(SMO AAA :o) TI
ou} B-) :@) CLABO:-) HHOJ Luv :
:/ OH WOT R :-) d:-) *:-) %-) GR
BK OTT WOM :-(SMO AAA :o) TI
ou} B-) :@) CLABO:-) HHOJ Luv :
GR8 {you} B-) :@) CLABO:-) HHO
) TIC :/ OH WOT R :-) d:-) *:-) %
Luv :-1 BK OTT WOM :-(SMO AA
GR8 {you} B-) :@) CLABO:-) HHO
) TIC :/ OH WOT R :-) d:-) *:-) %
Luv :-1 BK OTT WOM :-(SMO AA
GR8 {you} B-) :@) Luv :-1 BK OT
R :-) d:-) *:-) %-) GR8 {you} B-
OM :-(SMO AAA :o) TIC :/ OH WO
@) CLABO:-) HHOJ Luv :-1 BK OT
R :-) d:-) *:-) %-) GR8 {you} B-
OM :-(SMO AAA :o) TIC :/ OH WO
@) CLABO:-) HHOJ Luv :-1 BK OT

VIKING

Published by the Penguin Group
Penguin Books Ltd, 27 Wrights Lane, London W8 5TZ, England
Penguin Putnam Inc., 375 Hudson Street, New York, New York 10014, USA
Penguin Books Australia Ltd, Ringwood, Victoria, Australia
Penguin Books Canada Ltd, 10 Alcorn Avenue, Toronto, Ontario, Canada M4V 3B2
Penguin Books India (P) Ltd, 11 Community Centre, Panchsheel Park, New Delhi – 110 017, India
Penguin Books (NZ) Ltd, Cnr Rosedale and Airborne Roads, Albany, Auckland, New Zealand
Penguin Books (South Africa) (Pty) Ltd, 5 Watkins Street, Denver Ext 4, Johannesburg 2094, South Africa

On the World Wide Web at: www.penguin.com

Penguin Books Ltd, Registered Offices: Harmondsworth, Middlesex, England

First published 2000
1 3 5 7 9 10 8 6 4 2

Set in Chicago

Printed in Italy by L.E.G.O.

British Library Cataloguing in Publication Data
A CIP catalogue record for this book is available from the British Library

ISBN 0–670–91079–1

CONTENTS

EVERYBODY'S DOING IT...

Text maniacs everywhere know it's good to talk – but even better to text. It's fun ... it's simple ... and it's *so* addictive. Sending a text message on your mobile is the easiest way to chat to friends on the move as well as to say what's really on your mind. And here's how to do it.

So wot R U w8ting 4? GOWI (Get on with it)!

FOR STARTERS

The basics of text chat ...

Text fiends have created a whole new language of their own. And the more you use it, the more you'll get used to its strange little ways. The rules (if there are any) are:

1. Make words as short as you can, e.g. wd = would

2. Use a letter instead of a whole word where possible, e.g. u = you

3. Use acronyms (just the letters at the start of each word) for longer phrases,

e.g. FOTCL = Falling off the chair laughing

4 Spell words however you want if it makes them shorter, e.g. luv = love

Here are the basic words and phrases that are essential for messagers everywhere:

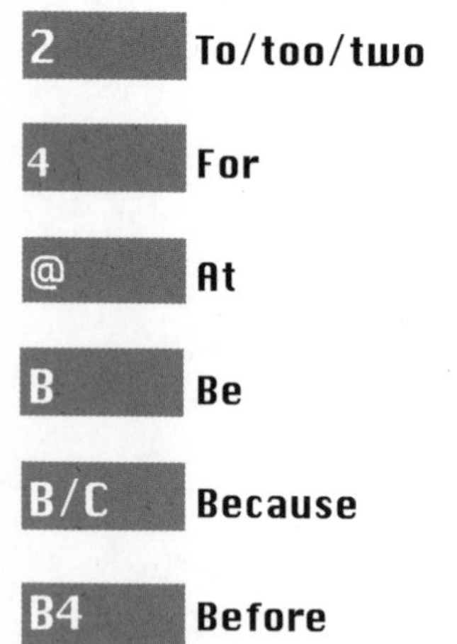

2	To/too/two
4	For
@	At
B	Be
B/C	Because
B4	Before
C	See/sea

Esp	Especially
F2T	Free to talk?
H2	How to
HVH	Have you heard?
IC	I see
IK	I know
OK	Okay
L8	Late
L8r	Later
M8	Mate
M80	Matey
Ne1 / Neone	Anyone
Neva	Never

No1	No one
Pls	Please
Ppl	People
R	Are
Re	Regarding
Spk	Speak
Sry	Sorry
Tho	Though
Thnq	Thank you
Thru	Through
THX TNX	Thanks
U	You
UOK	You OK?

UR	Your/You're
Usu	Usually
W/	With
Wan2	Want to
W/O	Without
W8	Wait
W8ing	Waiting
YM	You mean
YR	Yeah, right!

CUNNING PLANS

Got somewhere to go and someone to tell? Here's how to text those vital details.

2day
Today

2moro
Tomorrow

ADN
Any day now

ASAP
As soon as possible

ATM
At the moment

B4
Before

CU
See you

CUL CUL8R CYL
See you later

CWYL
Chat with you later

D u wnt 2 go out 2nite
Do you want to go out tonight?

ETA
Estimated time of arrival

L8
Late

L8r
Later

LMK

Let me know

Med

Immediately

Sec

Second

Soons

As soon as

U@

Where are you?
(You at?)

W8

Wait

W8ing

Waiting

W8 4 me at

Wait for me at ...

Wer r u

Where are you?

Will spk 2uL8r

Will speak to you later

MY THOUGHTS EXACTLY

Not happy? Want to express an opinion? Oh, go on. It's easy when you're texting.

AAMOF

As a matter of fact

AFAIC

As far as I'm concerned

AFAIK

As far as I know

AFAIR

As far as I remember/recall

AFAIUI

As far as I understand it

AISB

As I said before

AISI
As I see it

BICBW
But I could be wrong

BION
Believe it or not

BOC
But of course

BTA
But then again

BTAICBW
But then again I could be wrong

BTAIM
Be that as it may

BTDT
Been there, done that

BTW
By the way

CMIIW
Correct me if I'm wrong

CofB
Could have been

FICCL
Frankly, I couldn't care less

FWIW
For what it's worth

IAC
In any case

ICCL
I couldn't care less

IIRC
If I recall/ remember correctly

ILBT
I will be able to ...

IMBO
In my biased opinion

IMCO
In my considered opinion

IME
In my experience

IMHO
In my humble opinion

IMO
In my opinion

IMS
I must say

ISTR
I seem to recall/remember

IWBNI
It would be nice if ...

IYSWIM
If you see what I mean

KUTGW
Keep up the good work

MOF
Matter of fact

MTE
My thoughts exactly

NAGI
Not a good idea

OTOH
On the other hand

OTTOMH
Off the top of my head

OTW
On the whole

SAL
Such a laugh

SHTSI
Somebody had to say it

SSIA
Subject says it all

STS
So to speak

TBH
To be honest

TMI
Too much information

TTBE
That's to be expected

WFM
Works for me

E-MOTIONS

Want to express your feelings? This is how.

AAA Screaming

BG Big grin

BK Big kiss

CLAB Crying like a baby

DLG Devilish little grin

E2EG Ear-to-ear grin

FCOL For crying out loud

FDROTFL Falling down rolling on the floor laughing

FICCL	Frankly, I couldn't care less
FOTCL	Falling off the chair laughing
FUD	Fear, uncertainty and doubt
G	Grin
GBH&K	Great big hugs and kisses
GBH&KB	Great big hugs and kisses back
GGG	Giggle
GLG	Goofy little grin
Gr8	Great
Grr	Angry

HAK Hugs and kisses

HHOJ Ha ha only joking

HSP Highly sensitive person

IHTP I hate this place

JK Just kidding

LOL Laughing out loud/lots of love

Luv Love

NIDWTC No, I don't want to chat

NTG Not too good

OH Off hand

ONNA Oh no, not again

OTT	Over the top
ROFL	Rolling on the floor laughing
SMO	Serious mode on
SMOFF	Serious mode off
SUFID	Screwing up face in disgust
TGIF	Thank God it's Friday
TIC	Tongue-in-cheek
TIME	Tears in my eyes
VBG	Very big grin
VBEG	Very big evil grin
XInt	Excellent

Another way of expressing yourself is to send an Emoticon with your message – a little sideways face which shows how you're feeling.

:-II	Angry
d:-)	Baseball-cap man
*:-)	Clown
%-)	Confused
:'-(	Crying
:>	Devilish grin
:-Ló	Drooling
[:-(	Frowning
:/	Frustrated
8-]	Glasses

:-)	Happy/smiley
{you}	Hug
:-*	Kiss
:-D	Laughing/grinning
:-I	Not talking
:@)	Pig
@-‘-, --	Rose
:-(	Sad
0:-)	Saintly/angelic
:-@	Screaming
B-)	Shades
:-O	Surprised/shocked

:-p	Tongue-in-cheek/ sticking tongue out
:-&	Tongue-tied
:-))	Very happy
;-)	Winking/teasing

VIRTUAL HUGS

Like someone a lot? Tell them this way ...

Bf
Boyfriend

BK
Big kiss

F2F
Face to face

GBH&K
Great big hugs and kisses

GBH&KB
Great big hugs and kisses back

Gf
Girlfriend

GSOH
Good sense of humour

HAK
Hugs and kisses

HOYEW
Hanging on your every word

ILU ILY
I love you

IWBNI
It would be nice if ...

KOTL
Kiss on the lips

LJBF
Let's just be friends

LOL
Lots of love

Luv
Love

MAY
Mad about you

PDA
Public display of affection

SOVS
Someone very special

SWAK
Sealed with a kiss

TC
Take care

TLC
Tender loving care

VH
Virtual hug

Have a look at the Emoticons on page 24 for some other ways to send hugs and kisses.

ANY QUESTIONS?

An urgent need to ask, but don't want everyone to hear? Just text.

AWHFY
Are we having fun yet?

AYT
Are you there?

BAC
By any chance?

CHOWUR | CHUR
See how you are

Douth
Do you think ...?

DUCWIC | DYSWIS
Do you see what I see?

DYHWIH

Do you hear what I hear?

F2T

Free to talk?

HIB

Have I been ...?

HUH

Have you heard?

KWIM

Know what I mean?

PLMKO

Please let me know, OK?

RFC

Request for comments

RUOK

Are you OK?

U@ | Wer r u

Where are you?
(You at?)

Wadya

What do you ...?

WDYMBT

What do/did you mean by that?

Werv u bin

Where have you been?

Wot

What?

WoubIt

Would you be able to ...?

ANSWERING BACK

Here's a list of swift and witty replies ...

BOC
But of course

BTTP
Back to the point

By
Busy

BYKT
But you knew that

CB
Call back

CFD
Call for discussion

DK
Don't know

DTRT
Do the right thing

GA
Go ahead

GMTA
Great minds think alike

GOWI
Get on with it

Gr8
Great

GTBOS
Glad to be of service

HSIK
How should I know?

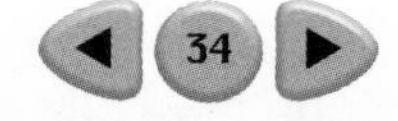

HTEI

Hope this explains it

HTH

Hope this helps

IC

I see

ICUR

I see you are

IDGI

I don't get it

IDK

I don't know

IDTS

I don't think so

IK

I know

INT
I'll never tell

IOU
I owe you

ITYM
I think you mean

IWIK
I wish I knew

JAM
Just a moment/just a minute

JAS
Just a second

LMA
Leave me alone

LMK
Let me know

LTNS
Long time no see

MTE
My thoughts exactly

NAGI
Not a good idea

NBD
No big deal

NHOH
Never heard of him/her

NIAA
No idea at all

NIDWTC
No, I don't want to chat

NL
Not likely

NLI
Not logged in

NM
Never mind

NOYB
None of your business

NP
No problem

NQA
No questions asked

NTIM
Not that it matters

NYP
Not your problem

O
Over (to you)

OIC

Oh, I see

OK

Okay

ONNA

Oh no, not again

OW

Oh well

PCB

Please call back

PCM

Please call me

PTM

Please tell me

RTI

Read the instructions

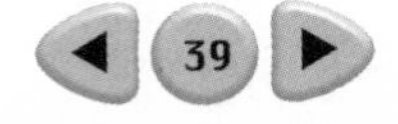

SCNR
Sorry, could not resist

SITD
Still in the dark

Sry
Sorry

SWYP
So what's your problem?

T4LMK
Thanks for letting me know

TFTT
Thanks for the thought

TWYT
That's what you think

TYLE
Took you long enough

URLCM
You're welcome

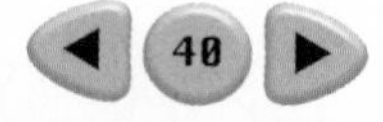

WB
Welcome back

Will spk 2uL8r
I will speak to you later

Xlnt
Excellent

YCBS
You can't be serious

YCLIU
You can look it up

YGTBK
You've got to be kidding

YKWIM
You know what I mean

HEATED EXCHANGES

Not impressed with what you're hearing? Tell the sender where to go.

CIO
Cut it out

DYOH
Do your own homework

EOD
End of discussion

FCOL
For crying out loud

GAL
Get a life

GL
Get lost

GOOML
Get out of my life

GOWI
Get on with it

ICCL
I couldn't care less

KISS
Keep it simple, stupid

LMA
Leave me alone

LTBF
Learn to be funny

MYOB
Mind your own business

NOYB
None of your business

OTL
Out to lunch

PMFBR
Pardon me for being rude

RTS
Read the screen

ROTBA
Reality on the blink again

SOHF
Sense of humour failure

SU
Shut up

SUNOILTY
Shut up, no one is listening to you

SWDYRTW
Since when did you rule the world?

SWYP
So what's your problem?

TAH
Take a hint

TINWIS
That is not what I said

TMI
Too much information

TSOHF
Total sense of humour failure

TWYT
That's what you think

TYLE
Took you long enough

TYVLYWEL
Thank you very little, you're welcome even less

WALOR
What a load of rubbish

WOWF
Witless one word follow-up

WYP
What's your point?

WYSOH
Where's your sense of humour?

YGTBK
You've got to be kidding

YHL
You have lost

YHBW
You have been warned

YOYO
You're on your own

SIGNING OFF

Here's how to have the last word.

ATB

All the best

B4N

Bye for now

BB

Bye-bye

BBFN

Bye-bye for now

BBIAB

Be back in a bit

BBL

Be back later

BBS

Be back soon

BCNU

Be seeing you

BFN

Bye for now

BK

Big kiss

BRB

Be right back

CB

Call back

CFD

Call for discussion

CU

See you

CUL CUL8R CYL
See you later

CWYL
Chat with you later

EOD
End of discussion

G2G
Got to go

GBH&K
Great big hugs and kisses

GGN
Gotta go now

GTG
Got to go

HAK
Hugs and kisses

HAND
Have a nice day

LOL
Lots of love

ML
More later

NN
Night-night

NRN
No reply necessary

NTDBWY
Nice to do business with you

OO
Over and out

PCB
Please call back

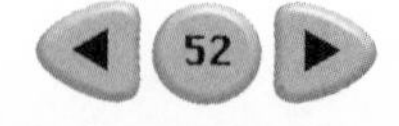

PCM
Please call me

Rgds
Regards

RSVP
Repondez s'il vous plait
(please reply)

TAF
That's all, folks!

TAFN
That's all for now

TC
Take care

TIA
Thanks in advance

TMB
Text me back

TTFN

Ta-ta for now

TTL4N

That's the lot for now

TTUL TTYL

Talk (or type) to you later

AND MORE . . .

Useful bits and pieces

24/7

Twenty-four hours a day, seven days a week

AFK

Away from keyboard

AIW

As it were/was

AKA

Also known as

AMAP

As much/many as possible

Attn

Attention

BIC

Best in class

BOF
Birds of a feather

DNA
Did not answer

DOB
Date of birth

DRA
Don't recognize acronym

DTTAH
Don't try this at home

EOL
End of lesson

FCFS
First come, first served

FITB
Fill in the blanks

FOAF

Friend of a friend

FTASB

Faster than a speeding bullet

FTL

Faster than light

FYA

For your amusement

FYI

For your information

GAFIA

Get away from it all

INPO

In no particular order

IOW

In other words

IRL

In real life

ISO

In search of

IYF

In your face

JFF

Just for fun

JIC

Just in case

LMC

Lost my connection

MOTD

Message of the day

NBTD

Nothing better to do

Ntl

Nevertheless

OAUS

On an unrelated subject

Ob

Obligatory

OBTW

Oh, by the way

OOSOOM

Out of sight, out of mind

OWTTE

Or words to that effect

PAW

Parents are watching

Pobl

Possible

POV

Point of view

PS

Postscript/Playstation

QED

Quod erat demonstrandum/
Quite easily done

RAK

Random act of kindness

RL

Real life

RNA

Ring, no answer

Sec

Second

SEP

Somebody else's problem

SW

Software/So what?/Says who?

TBA

To be announced

TBC

To be continued/To be confirmed

TNOTVS

There's nothing on TV so ...

TPAE

The possibilities are endless

VR

Virtual reality

WAEF

When all else fails

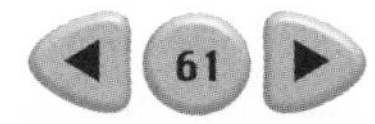

WOA
Work of art

WOM
Word of mouth

WOT
Waste of time

WSLS
You win some, you lose some

WWW
World Wide Web/
Why? Why? Why?

WYSIWYG
What you see is what you get

YA
Yet another

YANETUT

You are not expected to understand this

YHTBT

You had to be there

INDEX

O

P

Q

R

Y

*:-) %-) GR8 {you} B-) :@) CLA
MO AAA :o) TIC :/ OH WOT R :-
LABO:-) HHOJ Luv :-1 BK OTT W
-) d:-) *:-) %-) GR8 {you} B-) :@)
-(SMO AAA :o) TIC :/ OH WOT R
LABO:-) HHOJ Luv :-1 BK OTT W
-) d:-) *:-) %-) GR8 {you} B-) :@)
-(SMO AAA :o) TIC :/ OH WOT R
LABO:-) HHOJ Luv :-1 BK OTT W
-) d:-) *:-) %-) GR8 {you} B-) :@)
-(SMO AAA :o) :-) d:-) *:-) %-) G
-1 BK OTT WOM :-(SMO AAA :o) T
you} B-) :@) CLABO:-) HHOJ Luv
OH WOT R :-) d:-) *:-) %-) GR8
BK OTT WOM :-(SMO AAA :o) T
you} B-) :@) CLABO:-) HHOJ Luv
OH WOT R :-) d:-) *:-) %-) GR8
BK OTT WOM :-(SMO AAA :o) T
you} B-) :@) CLABO:-) HHOJ Luv
OH WOT R :-) d:-) *:-) %-) GR8
BK OTT WOM :-(SMO AAA :o) T
you} B-) :@) CLABO:-) HHOJ Luv
OH WOT R :-) d:-) *:-) %-) GR8
BK OTT WOM :-(:-) d:-) *:-) %
uv :-1 BK OTT WOM :-(SMO AAA
GR8 {you} B-) :@) CLABO:-) HHO
) TIC :/ OH WOT R :-) d:-) *:-) %
uv :-1 BK OTT WOM :-(SMO AAA
GR8 {you} B-) :@) CLABO:-) HHO
) TIC :/ OH WOT R :-) d:-) *:-) %
OM :-(SMO AAA :o) TIC :/ OH W
@) CLABO:-) HHOJ Luv :-1 BK OTT
:-) d:-) *:-) %-) GR8 {you} B-)
OM :-(SMO AAA :o) TIC :/ OH W
@) CLABO:-) HHOJ Luv :-1 BK OTT
:-) d:-) *:-) %-) GR8 {you} B-)